In the Heart of the Red Sea

Text by Raja Alem

Illustrations by Giulia Masia

My name is Nahham and this is my uncle Khashkhash.

"Khashkhash, what a funny name! I have only known you under this name, uncle."

My uncle laughs. "It's an ancient name pirates gave me. It reminds them of the Andalusian admiral and adventurer who sailed across the Sea of Darkness and reached the American continent before Columbus."

My uncle is an adventurer who loves the sea and he is the one who called me Nahham. When he heard me sing one day, he told me: "You have a sweet voice: I shall call you Nahham. It's a name we give in the Arab Gulf to sea shantymen whose singing brings joy to sailors' hearts."

My heart grew fond of the sea, and I began to spend my school holidays in Jeddah at sea with my uncle.

I love nights spent at sea, especially when my uncle stops the boat's engine and lets the boat float freely.

One night, Nahham and his uncle sat at the edge of the boat listening to the universe.

Everything was quiet except for the sound of small waves gently licking the hull of the boat. The boat rocked gently, and the air made them drowsy.
They retired early to their cabin which was situated in the front part of the boat.

That was the second night that Nahham woke up to a warm gentle touch across his body. But tonight, he was unable to resist the feeling of something pulling him out to the deck.

He got up quietly, not to wake his uncle, and went out.

When he stepped out of the cabin, his eyes fell on a strange scene. Around the boat colorful lights moved beneath the sea surface. It was phosphorescent fish jumping happily in the air.

Nahham's heart beat with excitement. He had never felt like this before. Bewitched, he went down the stairs leading to the water. He was not used to swimming at night without his uncle, but the dancing of phosphorescent fish erased all his fears. As he got into the water, he felt the warmth of the fish.

These were no ordinary fish, they were fish made of a warm tickling light, and they pulled him away from the ship. He only realized that he was far away from the ship when he could no longer see lights and the sea was quiet.

Out of the dark waters appeared a stinger fish. It stung him with its tail, *tsshhk*, and made him sink into the water.

As the water began to fill his lungs and his body faltered, Nahham realized that he was drowning. The more he tried to save himself, the more he sank into the depths of the sea.

All of a sudden, a voice came from the depths of the sea: "Fear nothing Nahham, breathe from your heart, and trust its strength. The heart is connected to God. Surrender to the sea."

Nahham plucked up his courage and surrendered to the sea.

The voice wrapped him in a bubble of softness, and he no longer felt like he was choking. It comforted him: "Don't be scared. At a depth of two hundred meters, you won't be able to see anything. It will be dark, but I'll guide you with my light."

The bubble swept him away through whirlpools and caves, until they arrived at a circle of reef corals that looked like a meadow.

There, a giant water creature appeared, featureless, just like a cloud. "It is I who called you," he said.

Nahham realized that it was the water talking to him. And not in a human language, but in a language only understood by the heart.

"I am Genius Loci."

"Genius Loci?"

"Yes, the protective spirit of the Red Sea. I have chosen you to help guard it."

Nahham stood bewildered in front of the water creature and amazed at the offer made to him.

"It's absolutely impossible! How can I guard a mighty creature such as the sea?"

"By watching, by opening your heart, by learning and then sharing what you learn about our marine world with your friends. You are the future, and we need your help."

Nahham didn't know what to say.

The Genius Loci laughed and imitated Nahham: "'It's absolutely impossible!' Allow the sea to introduce itself to you."

Out of nowhere, cyanobacteria (blue-green algae) darted towards Nahham, *whoosh*, and stained his body which turned shimmering red.

Genius Loci smiled. "These are the sea's red blood corpuscles," he said.

"Are they the reason the Red Sea is red?"

"They don't dye the sea, but along with the sun they give it a red reflection. The Red Sea is a mirror that reflects your image. Look to the north, what do you see?"

"I see the reflection of a red desert and red mountains on its western shores. And I see you, Genius Loci, your red reflection. That's funny," Nahham answered.

"You seem to like stories, so I will tell you a nice one. I look like this because I lived on the red planet of Mars. I left it thirty million years ago for Earth, because I longed for water, and I landed in the Red Sea. It was one mighty landing. It made volcanoes erupt, *boom splash!* and caused this gap that separates Asia and Africa. Then the rain came and filled it with water."

The story was told with such enthusiasm that a current swept Nahham away and made him swirl like a revolving cup in an amusement park.

"How exciting! It's absolutely impossible! I can't believe that I have met a Martian!"

"All beings are the same, we all carry stardust within us."

The Genius Loci carried Nahham in his cloud and dove to the bottom of the sea.

"Look, the volcano craters are still here."

Oooooh, strong vibrations from the craters hit Nahham... *Ziiit ziiit*, Nahham felt as if the Genius Loci was tickling him with these jerks.

"That thumping sound is actually small quakes that start in the cracks made by volcanoes in the crust of the earth."

"That's absolutely impossible! I think aliens are doing the thumping. It seems like a dangerous thumping too."

"It isn't dangerous anymore, because the volcanoes are dormant and their eruptions are minor. They're more like giggles. But their existence proves that the Red Sea isn't just some skinny sea."

"Haha, volcanoes that giggle?"

"Can I tell you a secret? The volcanoes and I make the Red Sea widen at an average of 2.17 cm every year. We do that to bring out the ocean it holds within."

"Unbelievable! My friends will never believe that you widen the sea. You really are a strange Martian."

The Genius Loci laughed, and his laugh made waves that reached the surface of the sea and shook passing ships.

"I would like you to get to know our Red Sea's creatures. And they are ready to meet you."

Nahham's heart leapt with joy as they passed through endless fields of gold, shimmering blue, green, and red coral reef.

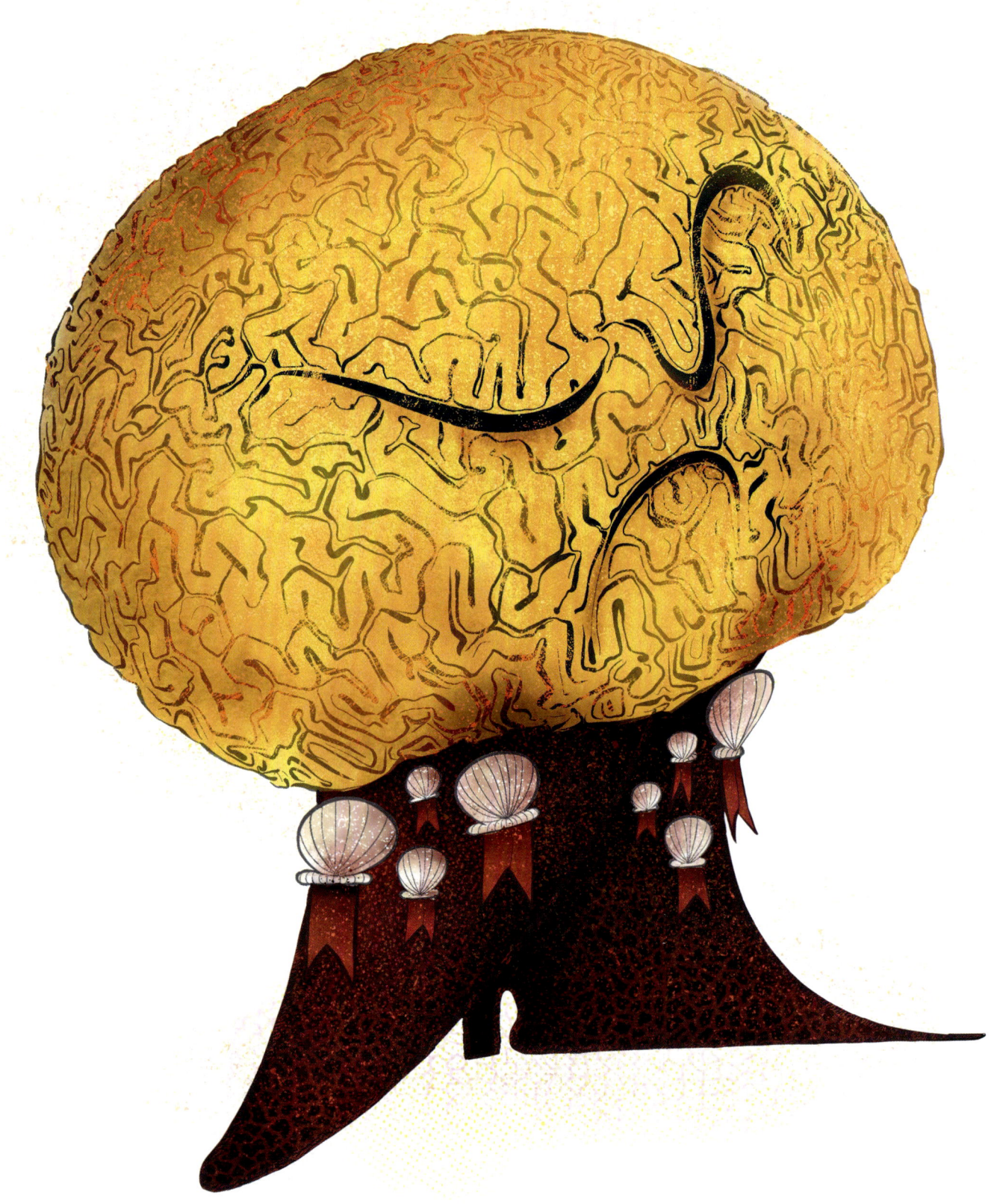

A strange scene drew his attention.
"Wow! Look, an alien's head!"

"That's the Brain Coral. He's the chief guardian of the sea. He thinks hard and sends his thoughts into the sea."

He introduces Nahham to the coral: "Meet Nahham, we'll be adding him to our team of guardians."

The Brain Coral shook, sending electric waves. "Let me think about it," he said.

Suddenly the sea became quiet.

The Brain Coral then said: "Here is a negative thought: it's not wise, Genius Loci, to choose such a small creature to guard the sea."

He turned to Nahham inquisitively and said: "How old are you, human?"

"Nine years old," stammered Nahham.

"Haha, I am seven thousand years old, and the sea is thirty million years old. You are only nine, and you think that you can be a guardian?"

Nahham wanted to explain to the Brain Coral that it wasn't his idea, but the Brain Coral turned to the Genius Loci and said: "Here is another negative thought: human beings are the biggest threat to the sea, and you go and choose a human to guard it?"

The Genius Loci replied calmly: "Your thoughts about humans being a danger are correct. This human may seem small, but he's very powerful, and he can use his power to protect the creatures of the sea."

The coral scratched its head. "Hmm, that's a good idea," he said.

He turned to Nahham and said: "Here's an awkward question: what do you know about corals?"

Nahham answered timidly: "Corals are sea creatures that look like rocks and plants."

"Haha, your knowledge of corals needs reinforcement. I have a positive suggestion: there's a science class at the School of Sea Corals. You will learn a lot from Mrs. White Venus Fan Coral's class.

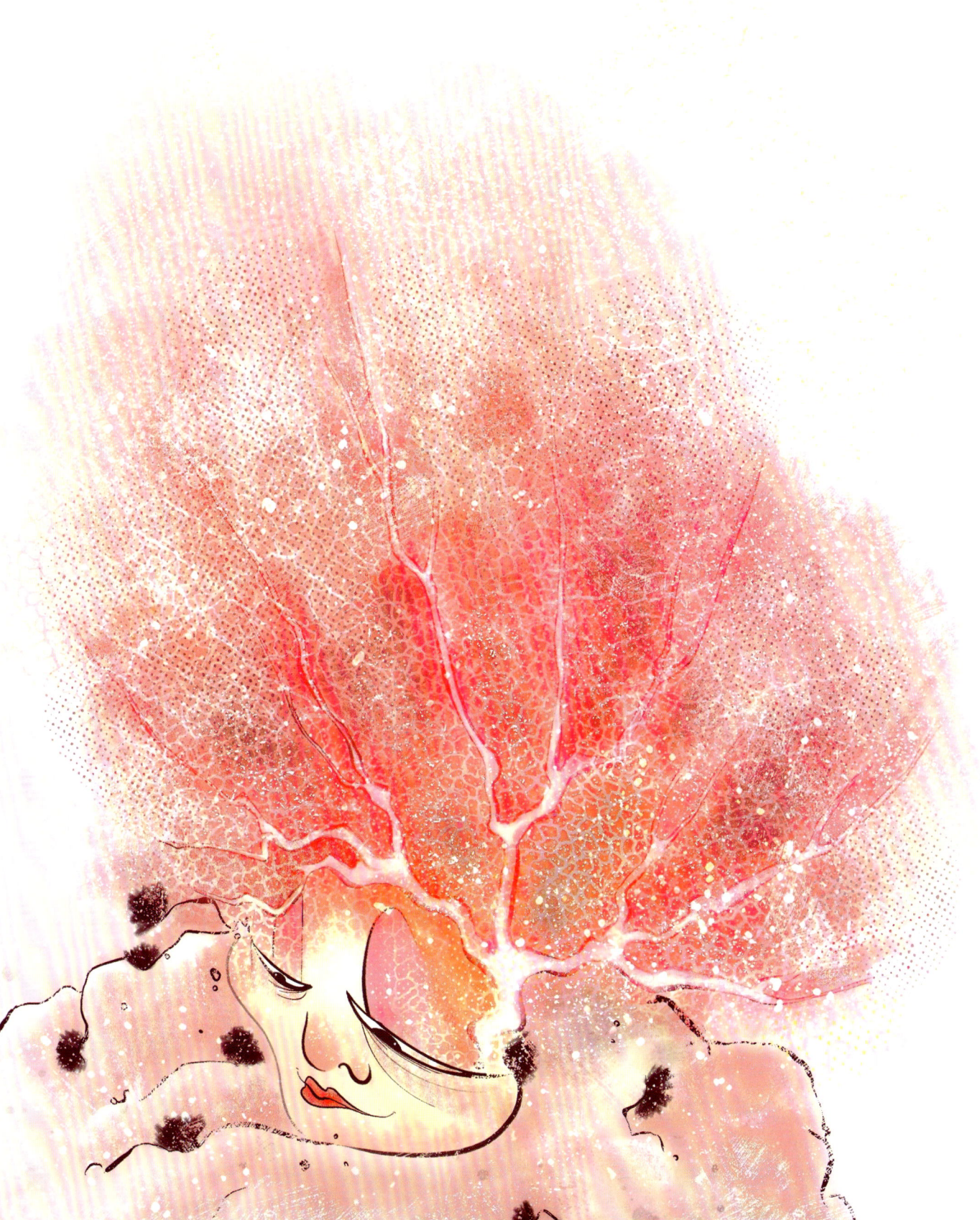

The Genius Loci dove with Nahham through varieties of soft and hard pink, red, purple, white, and black corals.

"How exciting! Is this an underwater honeycomb?"

The Genius Loci smiled. "It's a Honeycomb Coral, a honeycomb for fish, not bees," he replied.

He led Nahham under corals that looked like leaves.

"Unbelievable! Strawberries in the sea?"

The Genius Loci laughed and answered: "They look like strawberries. There are others that look like lettuce and broccoli. Just like in a vegetable market."

He suddenly warned him: "Watch out for the Fire Coral, it protects itself by stinging anything that comes close."

They finally arrived at the school.

Nahham found himself in Mrs. White Venus Fan's classroom. Groups of fish and corals were spread out upon the sand.

A group of bright yellow and orange Sun Corals drew close to Nahham and touched him carefully with their tentacles that expand at night.

The teacher said: "This is our guest Nahham. He's here to learn about our sea." The fish peered at him curiously.

The teacher then said: "And now, a moment of silence. Let's feel the sea." They all closed their eyes, and the teacher whispered: "Feel the warmth, the Red Sea is one of the warmest seas. Heat is important, because it preserves the diversity of marine life."

Nahham felt deep warmth that reminded him of the touch of his mother's hand.

"Now, we shall begin the class."

On the board she wrote: "Remember that there are two hundred and fifty types of coral in our Red Sea."

The Yellow Guinea Fowl Puffer Fish who was swimming nearby, proudly added: "Twenty of the Red Sea corals are rare and exist in no other sea."

The teacher patted him with her colorful fan. "You really are a genius with numbers," she said.

She wrote what he said on the board then asked the class:

"Now, who wants to give a brief summary of the agreements signed by the corals?"

The Whip Coral got up and wrote with his long red whip:

"The coral is an animal that doesn't move, it is deeply rooted in the sea floor. We, corals, have agreed with the algae to work together to build the biggest living ecosystem on earth."

"A living ecosystem? Imagine that your home breathes, eats, grows and has an extra room here, a balcony there added to it every day. Impossible!"

The Mushroom Coral with his claws jutting out of its mouth added:

"We corals have strong body structures. They are the number one guardians of life on earth. With our chests we prevent strong waves and cyclones from destroying cities by the sea."

The Sun Coral enthusiastically added:

"We corals provide fishermen with fish and offer divers lovely sights."

The Star Fish laughed and said: "I am a star that loves performing. I could be an amazing movie star. I can take off an arm and replace it with another."

The teacher responded angrily: "Really! The star of our sea dreams of being a movie star."
The Star swayed her arms as she danced gracefully.

The Lizard Fish intervened, catching the teacher's attention. "Without corals we fish would lose our homes and would be swallowed by the deep sea," he said.

The Scorpion Fish shuddered and added: "The fishermen wouldn't find anything to catch, and millions of people would go hungry."

The Zebra Fish came forward and wrote on the board: "This is our agreement with the corals: the corals engineer hiding places and caves for us fish to live in, away from strong sunlight and big fish."

The teacher asked: "And now, who can sum up the number of fish in our sea?"

"My God, all this information is so boring," said the Round Fish, blowing air bubbles from her gills. She yawned and folded her frilly dorsal fin.

"In beauty contests they won't just judge you on your looks, they will also test your culture and your intelligence," said the teacher.

The Genius Loci whispered to Nahham: "Every year, this Butterfly Fish wins the sea fish beauty contests."

Nahham thought to himself: "What happens in the sea is no different from what happens on earth and in the sky."

Paf paf! From his stone seat the intelligent and naughty eight-armed octopus interrupted them. Two of his arms teased the Spider Shell, two others were wrapped around Nahham's leg, tickling it, while four wrote on the board: "There are one thousand two hundred varieties of fish, two hundred and four of which only exist in our Red Sea."

The small Thresher Shark was busy looking through his books and papers.

"Tell us Thresher Shark, how many types of your kind are there in our Red Sea?" asked the teacher.

"Forty-four types," he answered without looking up. He went back to reading his book.

The Chicken Fish became enthusiastic: "Hey, have you forgotten the terrifying fish of the deep waters?" he asked.

The Thresher Shark corrected himself: "Forty-two terrifying fish," he said.

The Chicken Fish flaunted his knowledge: "And the Giant Moray."

The Thresher Shark cleared his throat and said: "The Moray is just a slimy eel."

"But I saw one swallow a shark," said the Chicken Fish.

"Ah, well we're not sure about that," replied the Thresher Shark.

"And the Sun Fish, a lazy fish that doesn't swim but leaves itself to be carried by the sea current. It may be lazy, but no other creature can lay as many eggs as it can," added the Chicken Fish.

The teacher asked: "How many eggs?"

The Chicken Fish hesitated, so the Thresher Shark quickly answered: "Three hundred million eggs, in one go." The fish laughed.

The Chicken Fish whispered something to the stealthy Seahorse, and the Seahorse burst with laughter. This made the teacher demand: "What do you find funny?"

The Seahorse timidly answered: "It's the Chicken who's being naughty, not me."

The teacher smiled and said: "Now, what's going on Chicken Fish?"

The Chicken Fish said: "The giant fish impress you, but there are small sea creatures that are way more intelligent than they are."

Mrs. Venus Fan complimented him. "Well done, Chicken, all sea creatures, whether giant or small fish or even bacteria, are amazing. For example, look at this genius fish on Zoom."

A yellow Clown Fish with a belt and a blue collar appeared on the screen. It was no bigger than a finger and moved incessantly between the pipettes of the Sea Anemones.

The Clown Fish tapped on the screen to get Nahham's attention: "Nahham, I live in the poisonous Sea Anemones. No one can follow me here, I am safe," he said.

Nahham asked, amazed: "How come the poison in the corals doesn't kill you?"

"My body has developed an antidote," the fish replied.

The teacher added: "Humans can learn lot from this brilliant chemist."

Nahham's admiration for the Clown Fish made a small fish that was no longer than seven centimeters jealous. She said: "Excuse me teacher. I would like to ask the Clown Fish a question."

The teacher answered, encouragingly: "Of course, Skinny Cheek Lantern Fish. Nahham, this is another genius of the sea."

In her shrill voice, the Skinny Cheek Lantern Fish asked: "Tell me Clown, do you ever leave your coral and travel far away?"

"No, I only go out to participate in festivals."

"You prefer safety to travel, while I migrate daily. I migrate at sunrise from the surface of the sea to its depths. There, my secretions provide thousands of fish with food. At sunset, I swim back up to the surface and feed on phytoplankton. I chose to have daily adventures, I chose freedom, while you chose safety and remained locked up in the coral."

In a fit of spite, the Clown Fish made a leap that made the coral and the fish storm with laughter.

"Wooaah, did you see that leap, Lantern Fish? When I am alone, I think. My mind travels and I invent these funny moves which fill the sea with joy. You are an adventurer, have you tried fun adventures? Inventing something funny is the most difficult thing. Laughter refreshes the heart and makes it creative," he said.

The Skinny Cheek Lantern Fish shook her head, embarrassed.

The teacher intervened saying: "The sea itself is a genius. Look, I'll introduce you to brine pools existing at one thousand seven hundred and seventy meters beneath sea level. There are four in the northern part of the Red Sea that are unlike any other brine pools in any other sea. Unfortunately, we can't visit them. Anyone who enters them dies, they are extremely salty and contain no oxygen. And of course, where there is no oxygen, there is no life."

On the screen, the teacher showed pictures of the pools.
"In 2020, the sea revealed the secrets of these pools to human scientists, because humans thought that they contained no life.
In fact, there is a miracle here: sea creatures such as eels, big sharks, flatfish, and shrimps live there without oxygen. Your scientists are studying it to see how life without oxygen is possible. If you discover the secret, Man will be able to live in the sea and on other planets with no oxygen," she said.

"That's absolutely impossible! Life without the need to breathe?" exclaimed Nahham.

"Also, the bacteria in these pools can help cure serious illnesses such as cancer. The sea holds endless secrets," the teacher replied.

She added: "Do you know what they call the creatures that live in these pools?" The students were quiet. She answered: "The cleaners."
The students were astonished. "Yes, because they clean the sea floor and feed on the animals that die when they enter the pools,"
she explained.

The Pig Fish crept into the corals. "Ugh, numbers and information are bad for my brain," he grumbled.

The teacher laughed and hit him gently with her fan. "They aren't bad for your brain. The brain is an amazing machine that the sea has worked on developing for four billion years," she said.

"I have good news that will make you proud of our Red Sea," she said. They all pricked their ears.

"Life on Earth is under threat, because of its rising temperatures. This will lead to many creatures dying. Only those who can adapt fast to the rise in temperature will be able to survive."

The Pig Fish fidgeted and interrupted her. "Good news? This news is depressing," he said.

"The coral is used to an average temperature of 27°C, and dies if the heat increases as much as one degree. Heat dries up and kills the algae that help the coral build their structures. Then the structures collapse. The good news is that the northern part of the Red Sea can be saved, because it is able to stand an increase of 5°C, meaning that it can bear water temperatures that reach up to 32°C."

The Pig Fish sighed with relief. "Thank goodness, now I can breathe," he said, making his classmates laugh.

"Do you know how the corals have learned to stand heat?" asked the teacher. No one replied.

"In ancient times, because of the heat, the northern part of the Red Sea dried up. From this tragic event, the creatures living in southern part of the Red Sea learned how to resist the heat.

When the northern part filled again with water, the creatures that lived in southern part migrated north and carried these new abilities. Nature has its ways of transmitting knowledge between its beings to protect them from extinction."

She added: "In the future, if ever the seas and their creatures die, our Red Sea will be an international refuge for marine life diversity. All creatures from the seas all over the world will want to live here."

The teacher noticed that the Black and White Sea Krait had stiffened. "What has happened to you, Krait? We are used to seeing you slide among us. Why are you not moving?" she asked him.

The Krait didn't answer. He pointed carefully, with his tail, to his computer. On the screen an Arabian Picasso Fish appeared working in his workshop. He was busy sculpting a Krait between the stems of black coral.

Picasso addressed the teacher: "The Krait is keeping still because he is modeling for me. I am making a cubist sculpture as part of my studies of fish shapes and scales."

Nahham cried out: "What a thrilling project!"

"Nahham, note that fish come in colors, stripes, spots just like shore animals. Their beautiful color combinations have inspired artists worldwide and have inspired me to work with colors other than blue and pink," said Picasso.

The teacher said, encouragingly: "We are excited to attend your next exhibition, Arabian Picasso."

"You have underwater art exhibitions?" asked Nahham, surprised.

"Of course, the sea is the first and greatest artist, its art gallery is open to all. And you, Nahham, are welcome in my workshop anytime, if you are interested in seeing my new statue which is made of glass fish and fish scales. I am particularly interested in scales. They are the fish's armor that protect them from cuts," replied the Arabian Picasso Fish.

The teacher left after saying: "Don't let the waves wash away everything you've learned today, especially you, Writing Fish. You shall all pass a test when the moon is full."

The Writing Fish nodded and added what was written on the board to his memory.

The teacher turned to the Blue Indian Surgeon Fish and said: "Doctor, please send our best regards for a speedy recovery to our friends the White Corals when you visit them."

Before any of the students was able to copy what was on the board, the naughtiest fish of the Red Sea, the Masked Puffer Fish, ballooned up in front of the board and erased what was written. She was followed by screams of protestation, as she moved away with her mask covering her eyes.

The Rabbit Fish with a cut tail swam towards them out of breath: "Run, the Hedgehog Fish is coming with his frightening thorns!" he said.

The eye of the Hedgehog swelled reaching the size of a ping pong ball. "Don't run away, between my thorns lies a kind heart that looks for friends," he said. He went after the Rabbit Fish, and the Squirrel Fish followed them, filming the chase.

The Genius Loci and Nahham followed the Surgeon Fish to the field of White Corals, that looked like pale grey skeletons.

The Genius Loci whispered in dismay: "When corals are fearful, they fall ill and turn white. We call this illness the white plague."

"Coral are afraid and fall ill like us, and they die?" Nahham asked sadly.

"Everything around you is alive and has feelings. These coral fields are poisoned by pollution caused by humans," the Genius Loci replied.

"You mean the waste and plastic that we throw in the sea and on the shores?"

"Yes, and the acids and gases released from factories and machines such as cars and airplanes."

Nahham saw beams of light around the branches of the scared ill coral.

The Blue Indian Surgeon Fish came closer and told them: "Meet the rescue team: this is the Elementals Constellation."

A beam glowed and came forward to introduce itself: "We Gnomes are earth elements, and we rebuild coral colonies."

Another beam came forward: "We are the Undines, and our element is water. We ensure the corals' vitality."

"We are the Sylphs, and our element is air and light. We renew the coral's vibrant colors."

"And we are the Salamanders, our element is fire. We provide the coral with warmth to reproduce."

The constellation then left to finish its mission.

The Indian Surgeon Fish explained: "This rescue team works day and night to rescue the coral from the white plague."

"That's scary," said Nahham.

The Genius Loci tried to soothe Nahham. He said: "Do you know who the first person to be fascinated with the treasures of our Red Sea was? Bilqis, the queen of Sheba. I visited her in her sleep, just like I visited you tonight, and showed her the gold, silver, copper, iron, lead, coral, and pearls that our sea contained. The queen sent her divers to gather coral and pearls. She had jewelry made out of them. Nahham, we are happy to share our treasures with our brothers, the humans, on condition that they don't overdo the fishing and digging in the sea, and that they remember that even the sea can dry up and die."

The Genius Loci led Nahham to a racetrack at the bottom of the sea.

All of a sudden, a group of fish, some of which were more than three meters long, dashed in front of them at full speed, holding dotted rainbow-colored striped flags. They were silver, blue-grey, and purple, and Nahham found them breathtaking.

"These Sail Fish are our champions, and hold the title of 'Sea Killers,'" pointed out the Genius Loci.

The Sail Fish sensed that Nahham was watching them, so they got excited and began changing color. Their bodies turned blue with yellow stripes.

"The Sea Killers have been trained for the Fastest Fish Formula races. Their speed can exceed 110 km per hour."

Nahham thought the Genius Loci was joking when he said: "We are thinking of participating in the championship of the world's saltiest sea, because our Red Sea is 35% salt. But we would only win the silver medal. The Dead Sea would win the gold medal."

Nahham said jokingly: "Haha, a championship for salt dissolving in water?"

"The sea holds a combination of salts such as sodium chloride, magnesium sulfate, calcium sulfate, and bicarbonate, which are useful to the growth of corals and to Man's health," he explained. "And now, are you ready for the surprise that we have prepared for you?" he asked Nahham.

Nahham clapped his hands in excitement: "I love surprises," he answered.

The Genius Loci then immediately led Nahham to a huge theater filled with fish.

All of a sudden, the Clown Fish appeared on the stage with his yellow belt and blue collar. He started doing backflips and acrobatic moves that made the spectators roar with laughter. They clapped their fins frantically, wiggled their tails, and flipped.

Then a big wave swept over the stage, washing the Clown Fish away, but a fish with a beak broke through the wave.

The Clown shouted, warning the public: "*Tweet, Tweet*, the Indian Bird Fish is coming. Close your eyes, he will try to kiss you with his long beak and yellow tail."

A cloud of happy swirls formed, and the fish made way for the Bird Fish and his beak.

The Clown Fish made a big leap in the water, and the swirls swept the fish away, making them scream with laughter. The ceiling of the stage was filled with red, blue, and white translucent Sea Lanterns that were followed by a school of Bullethead Parrot fish.

"*Bang bang!* This is no joke, we are firing bullets from our heads and putting out the Sea Lanterns." The Sea Lanterns laughed, defying the Parrot Fish with their glowing light.

The Genius Loci cried out: "Don't underestimate the sharpness of the Parrot Fish's teeth. They can scrape things with their beaks, pick algae from rocks, and skeletons of dead coral. Then, in their intestines, they grind materials that cannot be eaten, such as calcium carbonate, and spit them out in the form of sand. Parrot Fish alone produce 100 kgs of sand per year. And that is the sand that makes the beaches you love so much."

"That's unbelievable, a fish that manufactures sand?"

They were interrupted by the Clown Fish, exiting the stage after having excited the audience.

A Three-Spot Damsel Fish appeared on the stage.

A giant shell took the microphone to speak to the audience: "Dear guests, welcome to our festival which shall be animated by the Swish Swoosh Band. We would like to welcome the Lion Fish, the king of fish, and his counselors the Tiger Fish and the Humpback Whales."

"*Rooooaaaar*," answered the king of fish with flashes of light from his pectoral fins and his fancy white and red poisonous thorns.

"And now, are you excited to dance the Red Sea dance?"

The audience answered clapping their tails and fins with great enthusiasm. "*Swish Swoosh!* We love you *Swish Swoosh!*" everyone shouted.

The music began, and the Genius Loci whispered to Nahham, putting his hand to his chest: "Listen here, it is music you don't hear with your ears but with your heart. Everything around us emits music in the form of deep vibrations."

The band appeared, composed of Guitar Sharks, Horn Fish, Spinning Dolphins, Spotted Dolphins, Bottlenose Dolphins, Sun Fish, and Great Whales. The band began singing in a mixture of whistling, crackling, tweeting and bubbling, that sounded like echoes from outer space.

The music was so invigorating that the colorful fish, the octopuses and sirens in the audience started dancing.

The stripes on the fish standing to the right of the king shook and went wavy. The king cried out: "How strange, my minister the Tiger Fish is shaking! Are you cold or are you dancing the hip hop?"

The Tiger Fish answered: "You are a well-loved king because you can be serious and fun at the same time."

The Humpback Whales standing to the left of the king danced as well, and a school of Soldier Fish standing there to protect them joined the fun.

Nahham felt scales against his arm, and he too began to shake the hip hop shake.

"Hahaha, don't be afraid Nahham, stay cool like me, I am an Alligator Fish."

Nahham watched the Alligator Fish move away, dancing with the Splendid Crab.

On the stage, things got more exciting. A Spanish Dancer Fish with her sixty-centimeter frilled tail appeared, and began dancing around the band then joined the audience, which bristled with excitement.

Suddenly, Nahham found two big pupils stuck to his face: "Make way for the Emperor Fish and my friend the Napoleon Fish. We train at the School of History to become heroic characters," the creature said.

Nahham saluted the blue-faced Napoleon Fish wearing a military hat.

Then suddenly behind him he heard a question: "I am the Orange Barber Fish. Do you need a haircut Nahham? Do you like my finned hair?"

He pirouetted showing off his punk-like spiky hairstyle.

Nahham felt the Barber Fish's fins straightening his hair with a type of marine resin. Nahham laughed when his hair stood like Barber Fish's fins and said: "You are a terrible barber. Smile, I'll take a selfie of us with our finned hair."

The Trigger Fish followed him, with her phosphoric blue and green made-up eyes and lips. "Come on Nahham, let me fix your makeup," she said.

Nahham laughed and moved quickly out of her way.

The Trigger Fish went after the Masked Puffer Fish. "Come on, you need a lot of color. I'll add happy green to your earthy color," she told him.

"*Shush!* Don't blow my cover! I look like a rock, so I can catch prey and hide from any creature that may attack me," he answered.

They were interrupted by the strokes of a hammer. "*Clang clang!* How noisy you all are! End this party. I, the Hammerhead Shark, don't like fun."

"You can hammer from here till the end of time, and no one will hear you," the Nurse Shark mocked. She was hiding in a network of caves behind the stage, digging up the sand and making a sucking sound while she swallowed eels to which she added ketchup made from the poison of Stinger Fish.

The green turtles poked their heads excitedly out of their shells. "Help us flip! Our thick shields prevent us from dancing," they said.

The Genius Loci answered: "Your shields are like great drums that resonate with the music of the sea."

The Clever Octopus appeared laughing: "I am the ideal dance instructor. Come on, one, two, three, *hop hop!*" he said.

He held the turtles with his eight arms and helped them breakdance, flipping them, making them do backspins, and puffing a cloud of colorful ink to add fun to the dance.

Nahham got excited and danced. He found himself singing the sea song:

"The creatures of my small sea

are wrapped around me like a necklace

and my heart swings between its pearls like a moon."

Everyone stopped in amazement, then began swooning and dancing around him.

When he finished his song, he noticed the sharks around him, the Whale Shark, and the Dotted Shark. He then got scared, but wasn't able to run away.

The Genius Loci laughed and said: "Don't try to run away, my friend. Sharks attack when they sense fear. They don't bother people swimming peacefully."

Nahham plucked up his courage and took a selfie with the Whale Shark to post on Instagram. His followers will laugh when they see how tiny he is next to the Whale Shark who is as tall as a seven-storey building.

Nahham then noticed the Sirens around their queen.

"Sirens have soft hearts, they pick up the music of from the sky and dilute it in the sea. Love is the biggest gift one can receive from the universe, because it makes you more beautiful. It is important to open your heart to it and give it to all those around you, be they humans, animals, plants or inanimate creatures," said the Genius Loci.

Suddenly, transparent wings and blue balloons with stars fluttered over Nahham's head.

"These are Starred Balloon Fish and Angel Fish. They have come to celebrate your journey amongst us and your discovery of our world," said the Genius Loci.

Nahham was in awe in front of the pistachio-colored fins of the Balloon Fish: "My God! All this beauty in the sea," he exclaimed.

Filled with joy, he danced with the Salamanders. Then his body began to radiate the same light that woke him up that night on the boat and swept him away to the depths of the sea.

"Look, my body radiates light!" he gasped.

Everyone smiled and answered together: "Now you understand that all of us, you, us and all other creatures, turn into light when we see with our hearts."

Nahham sighed happily. "Nahham loves the sea, Nahham loves the light," he whispered.

"The sea is a great being and a brilliant engineer. Nahham, you must understand that seas regulate the planet's temperature, so that it won't catch on fire. When its water evaporates clouds form, and it rains."

Nahham added "And because there's water, there's life, for humans, plants and animals."

"Yes, without water there would be no life," agreed the Genius Loci.

"That is why I ask you and children your age to protect the sea," he explained.

"I am only nine years old. How can I protect a sea?"

"You are gentle yet strong, cautious yet brave. You are both intelligent and imaginative. Your heart will tell you how," he replied.

Nahham didn't know what to answer to that.

"Come, let's dive deeper in the memory of the Red Sea, until we reach the place where miracles live. You will then realize that you too are a miracle," said the Genius Loci.

He led Nahham through a dark endless tunnel. Nahham was amazed that he didn't need to breathe in such a dark tunnel.

They passed through a very dark area, where they heard bombs, explosions and ships sinking. Nahham got frightened, but the Genius Loci comforted him: "Don't be afraid, this is the memory of the British ship that sank here. It was bombed by the Germans in World War II."

All of a sudden, everything went still and the huge shipwreck appeared in front of them.

Nahham was surprised to see a group of octopuses lying quietly on the ship's cannons. "Sea creatures love peace," remarked the Genius Loci.

"All creatures hate war and love peace," answered Nahham.

Then they passed by huge hulls where eels and sharks had set home.

Nahham thought they would stop there, but the Genius Loci said: "These ships carry ancient treasures. They were commercial ships carrying antiques, oils, perfumes, and spices which still remain in their boxes. We guard them, until you discover them and uncover their secrets."

He then pulled Nahham away. "Now, I will show you the memory of Man's miracles. The sea will never forget them," he said.

Nahham felt the Genius Loci's strong grasp round his shoulders. "Get ready and stay still," he said. In the flash of an eye, he led Nahham through the tunnel of the sea's dark memory.

Nahham heard the rumbling of thunder then saw lightning striking in the darkness. The Genius Loci whispered: "This is the story of Moses's escape from Egypt."

The thunder and lightning lessened, and Nahham saw shadows running in the dark.

"Look, Moses and his followers stood helpless in front of the Red Sea. It barred their way as they tried to escape from the Pharaoh and his army who were right behind them. When Moses prayed God to save him and his men, that's when the miracle happened."

Nahham shook as lightning burst. "The Red Sea parted in two causing a terrible rumble. Giant waves formed and a path appeared for Moses and his followers to cross the sea.

They walked through the sea until they reached safely to the other side. There, God spoke to Moses, on Horeb mountain, in the Sinai desert. The Pharaoh and his army tried to follow them into the sea, but the waves closed on them and swallowed them to the depths of the sea," he explained.

This image from the past shocked Nahham. He felt a sudden flow of energy and light pass through his body. Then a mighty force projected Nahham like a bullet to the surface of the sea. He found himself in his bed on the boat.

The long hours he had spent in the sea's memory were just a glimpse of a bygone time. He came back only to find that everything was exactly as he left it a minute ago. His uncle was snoring in his cabin, the sea was calm, everything around him was silent, except for the light breeze.

Was it all a dream? He still remembered the skeleton of the Pharaoh lying at the bottom of the sea among the skeletons of his soldiers and old arrows, axes, and daggers. He still remembered the touch of the Genius Loci's arm around his shoulder, and the sound of his heartbeat thumping in his ears, *boom boom boom*.

Several hours passed, but Nahham was still unable to sleep. Then the sun crept into his heart. A golden sun promising a fresh new day.

Nahham got up and ran to the deck, screaming heartily:

"I love you, sea creatures, and I won't let you down."

With his heart he heard the Genius Loci say: "Remember, a long time ago the sea covered the earth. Life began there in the deep silent waters. The sea is the mother that gave birth to all forms of life. Now, you must protect this mother and take care of her. She is filled with beauty, but is vulnerable. I hope that the new generations will show this great mother love."

Nahham burst out into song:

"In my heart a song says,

we are one being,

one body,

we are the land and the sea,

we are the infinite space,

and the light of God."

The End

Khashkhash Ibn Saeed Ibn Aswad was a Moorish admiral and explorer of the high seas, especially the Sea of Darkness (the Atlantic Ocean), who reached America before Christopher Columbus. His adventures were documented in ancient Arabic books such as al-Mas'udi's *Reports from Time*.

In his other book *Meadows of Gold and Mines of Gems*, al-Mas'udi wrote that in AD 889 Khashkhash Ibn Saeed Ibn Aswad sailed from Palos de la Frontera in the province of Huelva, Andalusia across the Atlantic Ocean and reached a previously unknown land. He returned with a shipload of valuable treasures.

Some historians claim that Columbus made use of al-Mas'udi's maps when he set sail from Palos de la Frontera on his first voyage to the Americas in 1492.

Author
Raja Alem

Illustrator
Giulia Masia

Art direction
Luigi Fiore

Copy editing
Francesca Bovetti

Translation
Dina Lotfy

Edited by the Ministry of Culture, Saudi Arabia and Skira editore

All rights reserved. No part of this publication may be reproduced or transmitted in any form or by any means, electronic or mechanical, including photography, recording or any other information storage and retrieval system, without prior permission in writing from the publisher.

Printed and bound in Italy. First edition

© 2024 Ministry of Culture, Saudi Arabia
© 2024 Raja Alem for the text
© 2024 Giulia Masia for the illustrations
© 2024 Skira editore, Milan

ISBN: 978-603-92170-4-6
(Ministry of Culture)
ISBN: 978-88-572-4892-9
(Skira editore)

Ministry of Culture
King Faisal Road, Al Bujairi,
Ad Diriyah 13711, Saudi Arabia
www.moc.gov.sa

Skira editore spa
via Agnello, 18
20121 Milano, Italy
skira-arte.com

Distributed in USA, Canada, Central & South America by ARTBOOK | D.A.P., 75 Broad Street, Suite 630, New York, NY 10004, USA. Distributed elsewhere in the world by Thames and Hudson Ltd., 181A High Holborn, London WC1V 7QX, United Kingdom.